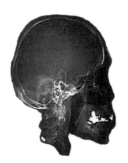

© Paul West 2006
© Lumen Books 2006

ISBN 0-930829-55-7

Lumen Books, SITES Books, and Helen Lane Editions are
imprints of Lumen, Inc., a non-profit, tax-exempt corporation
based in Santa Fe, NM and specializing in literary works, liter-
ary translations, and architecture as well as digital technologies.

Lumen, Inc.
40 Camino Cielo
Santa Fe, NM 87506
www.lumenbooks.org
Printed in the United States of America by Thomson-Shore, Inc.
Design: Dennis Dollens
Distributed by Consortium Book Sales and Distribution
11045 Westgate Drive
St. Paul, MN 5514
www.cbsd.com
1-800-283-3572

Tea with Osiris

BOOKS BY PAUL WEST

FICTION
The Immensity of the Here and Now
Cheops
The Shadow Factory
O.K. — The Corral, The Earps, and Doc Holliday
A Fifth of November
The Dry Danube: A Hitler Forgery
Life with Swan
Terrestials
Sporting with Amaryllis
The Tent of Orange Mist
Love's Mansion
The Women of Whitechapel and Jack the Ripper
Lord Byron's Doctor
The Place in Flowers Where Pollen Rests
The Universe, and Other Fictions
Rat Man of Paris
The Very Rich Hours of Count von Staufenberg
Gala
Colonel Mint
Caliban's Filibuster
Bela Lugosi's White Christmas
I'm Expecting to Live Quite Soon
Alley Jaggers
Tenement of Clay

POETRY
Tea with Osiris
The Snow Leopard
The Spellbound Horses

NONFICTION
Oxford Days
The Secret Lives of Words
Master Class
My Mother's Music
A Stroke of Genius
Sheer Fiction — Volumes I, II, III
Portable People
Out of My Depths: A Swimmer in the Universe
Words for a Deaf Daughter
I, Said the Sparrow
The Wine of Absurdity
The Modern Novel
Byron and the Spoiler's Art
James Ensor

Tea with Osiris

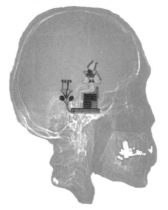

Paul West

Lumen Books

Tea with Osiris

1

Demure Osiris, stalker of the dead
and just about all else, may be said
to be the ultimate graves registrar,
though his ways are weird as samovars.
Nimble, he treks or sidles, skips
the light fantastic: heaven's own Astaire.
His lips breed elegies, his eyes are grief.
What, *we'd* like to know, is underneath?

Into time he flops, aping the pelican's
lucky dips. He charters ships.
He does not hedge with us or malinger
but stakes you to a blindman's death,
contorted miserable pop-singer
sucking in other men's breath.

2

Gabbing by phone to purge

his indiscretions (taking the young too soon,

deluding the old with dreams of surge),

he redoes an old lush tune

about amber waves of grain,

knowing what a swell he is. Complain

and his multicultural hand,

he may take you past all pain

and make you a pornographer in Maine

with seeing-eye like and brassy band.

You'd sooner or later expect a shootist

but not a SS Nazi parachutist.

He hopes only to meet *his* maker,

not some wave-hopping fakir.

3

In the next-door room a rough diamond
is choking to death on his own phlegm.
Moving in for the kill, Osiris kind of
says, "In a bad way. Think of it
in the psittacosis underground."
A candy striper says, "Not *my* patient."
Wrong answer: to Earth's bounty bound,
she suffers a chokehold insentient
as a kudu's rack.

Osiris is back! "Oh," chimes he, "for some vivifying
unguent to make the world smell sweet."
Among anorexic competitors vying
for fame, or fool's gold, Osiris works
his magic, disemboweling all Turks.

4

Osiris is sick. It *could* happen
to one so lethal even so, as plague
wolfs on the fold and pits their bones
or the *Zeitgeist* fans an ague.
A kidney stone has blocked his ureter
like a dead train aimed at Uttoxeter
or a crash-landed Cessna out at JFK.

So will he briefly go away
to toy with lasers, stents and what
Mostyn Blodgett, nurse, calls a Foley bag
of blood and pus?

And us. He is not away long, cutting wide swaths
through the surgic population. Wrath
has his day. Osiris wears black cloth.

5

"All's well that ends, you goys,"
(Osiris the econo-aphorist). "No news
good." Some medic's found
a fuzz on his heart valves,
pinprick from Goliath's elves.
So, after a three-day wait in lieu
he can have another Echo
followed by a Trans-esophageal,
such jargon a music to this beau
whose bladder's partly jammed
by stone somewhat smaller than
that blocking Christ entombed.
A wounded surgeon plies the steel.
Can this ogre be truly real?

6

Slimy how medics, born Joves,

obsess about the holes in us,

those treasure troves

marked No Exit, inventing gross

contraptions that shove or move,

widen, snip, and shuffle out.

Osiris gets his Foley catheter

like a perversion of Willa Cather:

down the penis, up the ureter,

held in place by a little balloon.

He also gets an alien thing within

on which to orate, all bared

on the condemned serial killer

whose rear, they crammed with filler.

7

So as, the story went, he wouldn't mess

the hot seat, but they wanted

a Michelin man whose ass

paid homage to grease,

or Sodom in reverse. All for Osiris,

torn penis evoking the fiery erections

from the stakes of the Inquisition,

the mangled tongue and throat,

the asshole's bloat.

Just what he needed to bring

him down a peg or two. Not Sing-Sing

(à la Benny Goodman), but in hospital,

which saved his turds and fluids, even spittle,

Osiris, ancient of days, gives not a tittle.

8

The point of this farrago

is that Osiris pleases himself,

open to suasion, bribes (see how far I go),

virtually inviting him in with his bloody

bris, but he never takes the bait:

couch potato on his eggs, broody

hen of war. He needs to wait

for the juiciest non-occasion

when all goes well, breeze

and prosperous voyage, no note

discernible, tow-headed children on deck

from A to Z, even Col. Lawrence,

Prince of Sands, an airman at his ease,

tending the seaplane tender.

9

Osiris is at it again. He always is,

stocking his granaries with fresh corpses,

his tiers with new souls. No pizzle

detains him from his wholesale haze,

though some have dodged his initial

overture (black pumps, teeth purple)

only to suffer onslaught from behind,

trapped by logic before they've sinned.

Never in their lives, they claim,

has their death and transfiguration

been so beautiful, seductive, tame,

the work of a cosmic artificer

with his mind on the job at hand,

accusations muted, all laughter canned.

10

How does he see himself? (Eschewing

mirrors of course). As a monster

of platitudes: an old bitch sowing

platitudes, lack-luster punster

with whimper not bang,

ego rain-sodden from

Rangoon, around the neck a Cang

from ancient China, from Brumm-

agem an ancient tin thumbstall,

between his toes enough Plasticine

to keep a thousand children sane.

An outline of a man, outrigger

alive there on catamaran,

agent of record for many moons.

11

You got to watch him. *Yougotta*

watchim lest he turn you terra cotta,

back to the earth earthy. *Chthonic.*

None of him is runic.

To Seth, e.g., he writes: "To Seth,

for death." Then sucks him dry

like a spider. Seth desiccated. Why,

who better to have rent him up

than this Heraclitean young pup?

That said, who's next in line

to polish off this porcupine?

Go kill death. So runs the ad

fishing for an upstart lad

not out of Houseman, sure. A cad.

12

Back in the hospital a child
of twelve is screaming, felled
by loss: "Where *is* she?"
They hold her close, then down.
Osiris added her to his own.
And the foam from her squandered lip
will take its place among famed
vapors from cuckoo to Lear, aimed
at schoolchildren out on a trip,
from Emily Brontë's poisoned menses
to Eva Braun's best *pensées*.
All grist for the Osiris mill
which says, whatever you will,
shall please me till I kill.

13

In civil terms, of course, Osiris
is the lord of misrule let loose
in "our" universe by death. Fire is
secondary here, but blood's the juice
of choice. You gotta give
to the bloodmobile of the new
apocalypse. You gotta divvy
up to the Osiris crew.

Glissando in urethra, he says,
one of the sublimest pleasures.
It seeds the loam, prolongs our days;
of all, the silkiest of seizures.
All balls to Seth, of course, who sees
dismemberment as the only reprise.

14

Behold the man of sundered mind

whose integrated cast was not designed,

the outcome being that, to speak at all

of this *lusus naturae* is to deal in shards

whose combination is the leopard's

out on the veldt beyond recall,

or even the Veldtschmerz, haunt

of other bewilderbeasts

unknown to Western analysts

of ciphers, enigmas, often missed

for being German or Hittite,

not that cipher smarts

lead naturally to sphinx's farts

or Osirian blackest arts.

15

On another hand, a man of bits.

Vietnam lieutenant fragged in the shits

by his own men and a grenade.

Thrice-golden ass of Apuleius.

Suicide refusing his own tamponade.

Brontë, E. afraid of death, so wanting to die.

Woolf with pocketfuls of pebbles: no use

paddling in the Ouse.

Hem's trigger, Crane's overboard leap.

St. Ex's *Lightning* dive. The big sleep

of almost everyone. Camus's tree.

The sleeping pills of me and thee,

none affects Lord Osiris, whose

beeline is a gross to be.

16

Those there are whose belief

is to morph him into autumn leaf,

Macbeth of the Nile, immobilizing

him: a major feat of downsizing,

open to cynics whose view of fate

is too euphoric to contemplate.

We go on dying, Osiris at work

upon us, no man's enemy, forgiving jerk,

whose lethality's a legend

mostly because he knits. "Perpend,"

says Polonius: think to the end,

then go suavely round the bend.

Others have gone before,

at Osiris's black bidding, as of yore.

17

He is to be found at the usual,

rehearsing bland imperatives; the beyonds

and the backs of them. Nothing

to scare the kids with, but soothing

non-stop: "Why don't you just die now forever?"

Some do, theists eager to touch heaven,

never having heard Ben's old

"Down is too hard." It sure is.

Those of us who look the other way

deny him all the time, limiting that siren bray

to the crystalline gaze of purists.

Yet how to convict the sonofabitch,

whose every move is flinch or twitch?

Head for Egypt? Stay abed? Bribe a witch?

18

Or head downtown to duke it out

like Coop? Corral his OK,

rope his snout,

give him the Boot Hill malarkey?

Shadowboxing all. He might listen,

his eyelids glisten, his teeth refang.

He might emit some chat

but what of that?

In the painful finitudes of Osiris's way

He'll get you, please, to go away

while he taps you for good measure

and recommends Bermuda leisure,

to settle the mind before execution—

one way of avoiding prosecution.

19

One day, Osiris, seeking aid

in what he thinks the non-arrival

of his bill, phones Verizon Survival

and mistakenly gets delayed,

then answered by a solicitous,

slow-going woman who spells everything

out: more courtesy than he to us,

and his heart goes ping.

In fact he has reached hotline

for the handicapped and is now

being asked not to be shy, and define

his degrees of blindness, deafness, loss of eye.

He catches on, and stammers his way into

imbecility, and the tom-tom.

20

Another side of him wears white gloves

as if at Westchester, not the place he loves;

the Boardwalk rained upon. He leers

at tourists, knowing he can have them all

for breakfast. Sunny side up, in oil.

He knows full well the volcano of desire

that sates him far too full: dead millions

when all he needs is thousands, choir

of mangled souls; he soldiers on,

vaguely aware of some abiding gyre

that always overdoes it and uses Osiris

as its baleful envoy, not for rhinoplasty

but something really nasty

such as a universe botched: a sty.

21

Where he is now, potent in a place

almost as gross as he, he lets

sound fade into melodic carapace,

a shuffle of fogbound Parisian cabriolets

never missing a beat

from the driptree joining his wrist:

constant unappeasable flick-flick

of chopper blades, searching out

a safe LZ, a spondee lost

yet hardly wiped out, memoir of colic

or some tidal bore yearning to spill.

All yields to the soprano squeal

of an emptied antibiotic bag, for real.

So frail a machine, but succor him it will.

22

At night he crashes into furniture,

all of it on wheels and wobbly

and so in constant Brownian motion.

He trips, tethered, his diarrhea,

écriture, explodes, an emulsion

viscous, tarry and all over the floor,

and for once he is helpless, crying uncle.

Somewhere he's lost his monocle

to all that intestinal asphalt,

not that he goes so far as guilt

while scrubbers and nurses toil

around him, scraping and mopping until

the scene (room 403) resembles

a shopworn abattoir. A crow ambles in.

23

As for the efforts of others

like mercury scumbled across

a mirror, he grudgingly covers

all of them with a blanket curse,

abominating the merely numerical

such as 911. He wants the bloodied face,

the amputated hand a thousand-fold,

one of your big-league thanatists,

no slinking miniaturist

not even by royal appointment

to the fiercest of the old pharaohs,

who, at home and abroad, chose

forthright butchery over disappointment

or any ointment, as everyone knows.

24

Pinned to the cork wall he finds

the slugabed victim's prayer,

one whole fawning stanza, there

to inspire the patient's mind:

God grant me the serenity to

accept the things I cannot change.

He snorts the snort

of a combined harvester, curt

and jussive, changes *change* to *abort*.

Better. Among killers he ranks

high, though inconspicuous, a born

duke of dark corners who'll adorn

many a portrait as the lone

rake about town, in his teeth a bairn.

25

And on. Also on the wall a big

blow-up of O'Keefe's poppies,

soft black calyx to squat into,

the huge sail-like petals mug-

shots of red windblown wimples

intended to smother the simplest

problems; bust them in two

if you like, a lyricism

put otherwise by Blodget's

"I miss the ocean!" engineered

in her by Georgia's reds

no doubt. Too far inland those beds

of smooth-thighed petals, too near

opium for guile. Osiris jeers.

26

Breakfastless, nervous as a newt,

he begins the word *Versed* without

sensing a pun there on the brink

of never-never. Let us say (or think)

All he gets out

is the first syllable and he doubt-

fully wakes up. "You didn't do it,"

sez he, "you chickened out. I gotta

pee, see, I just gotta, I gotta go."

Between his legs he senses a Rube Gold-

berg contraption, something between

a curtain rod and a turkey baster,

rigid, gross, all-penetrant pilaster

turning his *mons pubis* arsenical green.

27

What is this thing of sea or land?
Female of sex it seems. Planned
or improvised? Not so much a catheter
as, thanks to Weland the smith, a theta
doubled: rammed home
and up, cruising stratospherically
(and if you like lyrical assents)
up toward the meniscus or dome
of the heroic bladder chimerically
presiding over its own palace of scents
and the crushed, humiliated schlong.
All this, to help him pee his way
to glory while egging on the throng
to come and play.

28

Pleading his belly with the overlords

of surgery, he brings into play words

hitherto not his: *Gracious, obleeged,*

prevail, gentlemanly, and *liege.*

He pleads to have his catheter cut loose

but burns white-hot when a nurse

tugs from his johnson the long dose

of it, transparent and huge, an Alabama

white snake with a little bulb for head;

tinily inflatable if you know Norse

and don't want it to fall. A dead

faint follows. Some fellow brandishing paper

passes by. The paper unfurls in an aroma

of charred suet or dehydrated diaper.

29

When your music-lover goes sour,

when the deep purple rots away,

and mood indigo won't pour,

then Osiris turns against his fav-

orites, damning Dvorak the pan-Slav

of faked Americana, Debussy's come-

music, Ravel's sperm in your face,

even Delius's syph' aroma.

He wants them not to have written,

not even to have felt hit on

by phrases that shape a music's face.

As for the Rodrigo of Aranjuez

Osiris forbids the tale of its origins

on a dead piano in a shabby place.

30

Among the wilder imagings
of this period (Osiris ever up to date,
having had little radio, sedate
and tinny, sewn into his armpit),
there is the auto-da-fé beginning
with a dozen hijacked jets over
San Francisco doing maneuvers
before crashing into one another
or heedless towers in a pother
of smoke and soot, grist to his mill.
It could be an airshow, with Cessnas
and Pipers chuggily homing in. Etna's
roaring upchuck has nothing on this
rodomontade Oshkosh. Such his fill.

31

On the local front, a girl

screaming "Help me" and a bronchitic

stroke victim clearing cement from his throat

is all he gets, and would airily deign

to disembowel, or choke with trowel

wetted at the tap, imposed from above.

Sufferers go first, he sez, trove

of treasure, but unhurt souls may

also apply for coup de gracê and pray

for the fleeting tag of a poisoned boy.

Even when inmates howl in unison,

he resists, as a drunk might amethysts,

and lugs his armor south for benison

lest the sextons of the world resist.

32

Now and then he backslides:

having zapped his favorite Delius

he lets him back in for luscious brides

but not without a worsening *By Jesus!*

uttered to evoke the horrors of a fetid

brain that sinks *maladif* and clarted.

We are all his offal, writ into the sum

as menial conduits into kingdom come.

Did he apply? Was he elected?

Does he come militarily protected?

His eyes are dim, he cannot see,

he has not brought his specs to tea.

No: he just grew, like Topsy, born of

naught, destined to prevail. Torn off.

33

Make him what you will. Ruffian

sadist in a minor way, cosmic minion

to some, he's a twist in metaphysics

quite unlike other murderers. He sics

invisible wild dogs upon the innocent

yet prides himself most on those

whose patent virtue lacks all cant

and might expect deferment

for wild oats or being duller dogs

at work or play, cowed spirits whose blogs

dismay the internet as tepid torsions

in a putrid world. Only by extortion

does he forgive, slapping the recipient

with syphilis or other disease-docent.

34

One summer's day in winter
when the snow was raining fast,
a barefooted boy with clogs on
stood sitting on the grass.
He went to the movies that night
and bought two front seats at the back,
ate a big plain cake with currents in,
and when he'd eaten it he gave it back.

Flash there of that invincible childhood,
Le Grand Meaulnes or Forrest Reid,
learning etiquette for watching others bleed
and breech babies coming out suffocated.
Somebody loves him, sure, a vagrant wave
from a sullen sea, designed to misbehave.

35

Extravasation of urine from a kidney

blocked is what he suffers from.

A quarter-sized stone occupies one of

his ureters and has to be peed out.

Then nailed to his forehead, Voronoff,

his new, exotic name, he learns to pout

and throw his lumpy weight about

as if himself a plate tectonic

in a lifetime judged moronic.

He towers over all, needing no helpmeet

for the brain beneath his helmet.

Is he immortal then? Three hundred years

old like Janáček's vampire diva,

he lurks abed with a meat cleaver.

36

Would a fairy's kiss reform him?

No more death in this hemisphere,

sez Ariadne, couched on her island,

forlorn and suicidal. Enter Osiris, in fear,

to plant his banal kiss. A fair miss

by many a mile, it introduces him,

the author of butchery bacchanalia,

whatever you think of cutesy Naxos

full of intractable, violent hams

who'd love to do you in with faxes

adorned by Lon Chaney's pentagram.

"The way he walked was thorny"—Maria

Ouspenskaya—"through no fault of his own."

No crossing that old parallelogram.

37

"If our sweetest songs are those

that tell of saddest thoughts," sez Osiris,

"then our saddest songs are those

that tell of sweetest thoughts." Who's

asking? *I* am. It doesn't balance,

somehow it, doesn't add up. Dalliance

is verbosity. 'Twould be better

if we thought of something neater:

Our nightmares are what sustain us.

Blood and gore staidly restrain us.

Chancres and boils enlighten us.

The family next door are all dames

attempting a crosspatch lion's work

to which all the answers are horses' names.

38

Reports come in of innocents beheaded,

victims of an upstart Muslim lout;

Osiris appreciates the help of dreaded

tribesmen, longs to put their eyeballs out.

Impartial to the end, forgiving all,

he glows to hear from the dark Sudan:

falling-like-flies in one miracle,

wants there to be more, and sudden.

Not so much Dr. Death as Doctor Vibes,

death's passport stamper, stern to embrace,

strong to save, concocter of gibes,

who does all he can to end the race.

Those who curry favor with this lord

deserve his fervor, their plaint ignored.

39

While all falls around him

or at least enters the next phase

of decrepitude, he accustoms them to ways

of old or just developed, cherubim

and seraphim. To check his temperature

they slide his earplug out and then replace

it, business end in, as if that little aperture

were a cockpit kingdom and home base.

He asks for oxygen and gets it. Cocksure,

as the Versed fells him, his kidney stone

yields to the laser, which shreds it to dust.

They take out his catheter, quelling his lust,

and thoughtfully wheel him back where, alone

as a dolmen, he gnaws on the phone.

40

Fee-fi-fo-fum, he smells the blood

of human mites, a toe jam

to pop digital fingers in. A brood

of *morituri* make his proudest boast.

Sudanese matrons burn his toast.

Nothing is too much, not even

hell, whose counterfeit awaits him

with a tolling bell. "Take it in quim,"

he says, "I am a plague no doubt":

Gabriel to the drones in heaven,

Satan to the slobs without.

God help those that I unleaven.

In the course of shoving them about.

I am the heir to their estates. I rout.

41

He's improving fast, abler than ever

to bring the world to heel. His monopoly

of the living and the dead goes over

the top of tyranny, mortuary megalopoly,

and sets you wondering if merely

copping a feel at night-nurses is enough

to set him off on another rampage nearly

absolute, based on the Spanish influenza

of not long ago when folk weren't tough

enough to stand the fall cadenza,

of the germ that clobbered everyone's

forebears with an Osiris *fons*

et origo. Look up to him. He stuns.

"Teacakes for a million, all for me."

42

Assembled in the pall around him,

his acolytes—Buffy the Vampire,

Ursula Heim the Vamp, Connie the Quim—

look after him, extending their empire

only by a month or two as by luck

at Osiris's ghastly Ravensbrück.

They serve, but he takes them

down with glib *ars celare artem*

intended to discomfit others, whether

sycophants or drones, whose *joie de vivre*

wears a trench coat from the first,

hardly ever intended to weather

storms, insurrections, humble shivers

or the latest fatal Indian giver.

43

Strange to say, within the motley

crew awaiting oblivion, wrath's

jetty, there malingers a certain Seth

with notions of his own, his breath

illumined with coal-tar subtly

got up as mascara to persuade

Osiris not to stage another raid

from underneath, hauling folks down

into boiling sulfuric mud by their

labia, scrotums, and abundant hair.

Oh no, and not from above neither. Laissez-faire.

"Hey, yous," sez Osiris with a

patrician glare. "Hit is thee law,

you snits, come quiet or I'll claw."

44

All without implants or *faux* clefts,

just a casual business of power tufts

implanted by the deity at whim,

guaranteeing oversight of death's dim

latifundia. Not the slightest doubt

as to who he is: nurses tie

the tapes of his hospital smock,

ply him with hot water, for good luck

give him tiny insulin pricks,

and make his bed before his eyes,

a guy so "normal" he might go incognito

except for his golden helmet; a real beau

who winces on hearing "A real fruit"

in panic from the neighbor suite.

45

So you think pleading is best,

a grovel in one's junior years,

better to dare him, take him on,

mumbling, all your daily fears

bottled up as in some ship-burial.

He might relent for a year or six,

pock-marked muck-muck as he is on

his best days. Egg him on for sex,

he might go easy on you, ambrosial

well-to-do by divine charter.

Sometimes to be seen limping away

from some hell-bent encounter

with hyena, gibbon, leopard, cray-

fish, over whom he's the hunter.

46

You may well wonder at his

inconsistency, super-grass to the gods

while full of human foibles,

but it pays him to be both Attis

and Osiris; he actually shops gods

and their godforsaken *faiblesse*,

which is to say he's mostly mythic

without recourse to bloviated physic,

communion wafer, wine. He belonged

to the vast trade union in the sky,

his roar a thousand lungs,

his keenest act a regal obsequy.

Letters do not reach him, though

his lightning bolt can transcend snow.

47

Almost a catalogue not a style,
he mixes a pince-nez with rings,
wears contacts, lipstick, and Bing's
falsetto without guile.
Man about town, a face in the crowd,
he muscles on, bloody but unbowed,
co-opted quisling, smiling traitor,
he makes allegations, is the alligator.
Both backwards, but not backward,
he summons grace from nowhere,
then puts it back to charm the air.
If only he could trust us to obey
we'd love to while the hours away,
but we'd be trying to curtail dismay.

48

As fully languaged as Pan

with constant updates from the constabulary

of vocabulary, he stuffs his hoard

with hospital terms of the moment,

so much so that his outer garment

becomes one of words—Foley

bag, Foley catheter, "sharp bucket"—

useable nowhere else but enabling

this duke of dark corners to pass

muster, even when he sighs, "Fuck it"

or, in less censorious vein, ennobling

him elsewhere, as he says "Rolly polly

I will stay. Take your diet food away."

They do. He sighs. He dreams of holly.

49

Small things excite him endlessly.

A little mint he sucks has the same shape

as the rotor of the Wankel engine

and soon has him yearning boundlessly

for a car small as a mint. Some hope!

He would run it up his nose, honest injun.

This prankish side would endear

him to the hosts if only he'd let slip

a hint of it, but he says, "No fear:

I'll keep myself to myself

like an importunate, selfish elf,

Lord of the masses, breath of death."

Watch him for invisible diseases,

not that he gets the shakes or sneezes.

50

In one way he's as automatic

as one of those little tin speedboats

powered by an effervescent pill.

It means he's not dramatic

or climactic as he floats

in among us, but, mercy, he will

propel us to a mindless fate

no big Red Cross can mitigate.

You do not befriend this ogre

or stab him with an auger.

He's the out-personification of you

as mortified as blue or true,

and not to be copied in our jargon

as any standard type of gorgon.

51

Recouping, he rehears the patient,

obviously a connoisseur, who looks in

on him and exclaims "Aha, new faces!"

As if he were Osiris himself, a docent

superannuated and sleek. Earlier fits

come back to him: the young voice

screeching for her mother: "Where *is*

she? Where *is* she?" And the bouts

of echolalia ("Help me, help me")

suffered by someone else, a tocsin

to all Samaritans and nurses

to come running as if they are equerries

to the commander-in-chief of pain

who, told, won't let it happen again.

52

You'd think Osiris could be softened up,

but his very softness makes him

want you dead, free of all slop.

Then he can relax in the dim

aura of a job well done, all passion spent,

the victim shipped back home to Mom.

Not that he likes to cause an incident,

it's just his way of being innocent,

bestowing death and thus dispossessing

whoever it is of death's pain. Casuistry?

It might seem so if he were confessing,

but he abhors screens and palmistry

as blemishes on his morbid ministry.

He does not heed the concept missing.

53

As for Seth, building his anger,

he feels its volcanic rise within,

quite dispatching his usual languor

and drenching him in sin.

He lists Osiris's component parts

from head to tail, a roll-call

of useable assets to be put on sale

or sundered at some monster's ball.

The day will come, Osiris fragmented

by ax or cleaver, never to be cemented

together again, beyond the pale,

his death's-head vinegared by salt,

his trunk slit open, his limbs

lopped clean by automatic catapult.

Tea with Osiris • 115

Helen Lane Editions

Helen Lane was one of the world's foremost and most beloved of translators. To her more than 100 works translated from Spanish, French, and Portuguese, she added a model dedication to translation as practice, art, and spiritual endeavor in bridging the Dharma divide. She also stimulated other translators, beginners and veterans, in translation through her advice, editing, and example.

Helen left a bequest to Lumen Books for the publication of translations and exceptional new works. To that end we have established Helen Lane Editions in her honor and tradition. The first volume in the series, Diamela Eltit's *Custody of the Eye* (*Los Vigilantes*) was one of the last books Helen worked on.

We trust that this series will further Helen's life-long goals, and we invite you to join us in this project by contributing to the Helen Lane Translation Fund, Lumen Books, 40 Camino Cielo, Santa Fe, NM 87506. Lumen is a federally designated non-profit, 501(c)(3) corporation, and all contributions to Lumen are tax deductible.

Publishers: Ronald Christ, Dennis Dollens
Translation Editor: Héctor Magana
Advisory Board:
Peter Bush
Christopher Conway
Juan Goytisolo
Carol Maier
Margaret Sayers Peden
Elena Poniatowska
Paul West